Original title:

Luminous Echoes Against the Phoenix Wing

Author: Linda Leevike

ISBN HARDBACK: 978-1-80559-032-3

ISBN PAPERBACK: 978-1-80559-531-1

Specters of Firetouching Souls

In shadows cast by flickering light,
Whispers dance in the heart of night.
Embers glow with tales untold,
Feeding dreams as they unfold.

They linger close, these spirits bright,
With every flare, they hold us tight.
Through warmth and light, they show the way,
Guiding lost souls, come what may.

In the crackling hush, secrets sigh,
Memories linger, never goodbye.
Through laughter, tears, in fire's embrace,
We find our spirits in this space.

Past and present, woven as one,
Specters dance till the night is done.
With each heartbeat, they intertwine,
In flickers of warmth, our lives align.

When flames diminish, and shadows flee,
Still, the specters dwell within me.
Their essence, a bond that cannot sever,
In the hearth of souls, they live forever.

The Last Ember's Journey Skyward

A single spark ignites the dark,
With courage born from its small heart.
It flickers, sways, and yearns to rise,
As the night's embrace clings to the skies.

The ashes whisper, tales of old,
Of fiery nights, and heroes bold.
Through the quiet, it starts to glow,
A flight toward dreams where shadows go.

With every breath, the ember fights,
To reach the heavens, beyond sight.
Casting warmth through chill and fear,
Its journey echoes, calm and clear.

It dances upward, a fleeting flare,
In the hushed silence, it travels rare.
And in that moment, bright and brief,
It finds its peace, a sweet relief.

As the last ember fades through night,
A promise lingers, pure and bright.
In the cycle of flame, we learn to cope,
For even in darkness, there's always hope.

Harmonics of Fire and Renewal

In the depths, a rhythm starts to play,
The flicker of fire ignites the day.
With every pulse, the world takes pause,
Nature's song reminds us of cause.

Flames entwined with the whispers of wind,
A symphony begins, reigniting kin.
From ashes rise the flowers anew,
In vibrant hues, their beauty true.

Oh, harmonics of life, sweet refrain,
Through loss and pain, we learn to gain.
The warmth of fire, a tender touch,
In its embrace, we find so much.

From cinders born, a future gleams,
Fires ignite the strongest dreams.
With open hearts, we merge and flow,
In unity's arms, our spirits glow.

So let us cherish each note and sound,
For in the flame, our souls are bound.
In the dance of life, we intertwine,
Through fire and renewal, we brightly shine.

The Incandescent Song of Rebirth

In the silence of the dawn,
New life begins to stir,
Nature hums a gentle tune,
As hope begins to blur.

With each drop of morning dew,
A promise softly made,
The world awakens anew,
In colors unafraid.

Whispers of the winds embrace,
Carrying tales of old,
From ashes, dreams arise,
As the heart turns to gold.

The sun breaks through the gray,
Lighting paths once lost,
With every vibrant ray,
Rebirth comes at a cost.

So dance with gleeful grace,
Join the song of the brave,
For in each soul's warm space,
Lies the power to save.

Shadows Danced by Flickering Flames

In the hearth's warm embrace,
The shadows come alive,
Twisting forms in a whirl,
Where ancient spirits thrive.

The flames whisper secrets low,
Of stories lost in time,
Each crackle sparks a thought,
In rhythm and in rhyme.

Dancing close to the light,
The darkness feels the pull,
A ballet of the night,
With every flicker, full.

The hearth knows joy and pain,
In flickers, life unfolds,
From warmth comes every gain,
And shadows brave and bold.

So gather round the glow,
Let the stories ignite,
In flickering flame's flow,
Find solace in the night.

Glows of the Awakening Spirit

From slumber's deep embrace,
The spirit starts to rise,
A shimmer in the stillness,
A dance beneath the skies.

The heart beats soft with grace,
Awakening the light,
In whispers of the soul,
That banish all the night.

Colors blend and entwine,
In a symphony so sweet,
The world starts to align,
As old wounds find retreat.

With courage in each step,
The path unfolds with time,
A journey of the spirit,
One filled with joy sublime.

So let the glow be felt,
In every breath we take,
For in each heart that melts,
Awakening, we wake.

Radiant Feathers in the Night Sky

In the velvet of the night,
Stars like feathers gleam,
Each one a wish in flight,
A whisper of a dream.

They dance upon the breeze,
With stories left untold,
A tapestry of peace,
In silver and in gold.

Through the cosmic ballet,
We chase the fleeting glow,
In shadows, spirits play,
In the night's subtle flow.

With every twinkle bright,
Hope radiates its fire,
As feathers take to flight,
To lift our hearts higher.

So gaze at the expanse,
And let your spirit fly,
In this celestial dance,
With radiant feathers high.

Radiant Whispers in Celestial Flight

In the stillness of the night,
Stars begin their gentle flight.
Whispers of the moonlit glow,
Carrying dreams where shadows flow.

Velvet skies embrace the light,
Cradled in the arms of night.
Echoes of the cosmic song,
Guide the lost where they belong.

Shooting stars with swift intent,
Every wish a sweet lament.
In silence, hopes take to the air,
We find solace nestled there.

Celestial dances swirl and sway,
Radiant hues in bright array.
Embracing all that dares to soar,
A symphony forevermore.

In each whisper, spirits gleam,
Mingling softly in the dream.
Underneath the boundless night,
We become a part of light.

Glowing Reverberations of the Firebird

In the heart of blazing flame,
A firebird calls with a name.
From ashes born, it takes its flight,
Glowing shadows paint the night.

With wings that shimmer, bright and bold,
Tales of wisdom, soft and old.
Each note it sings a melody,
Of freedom's dance through history.

The world ignites in colors rare,
With every beat, the dreamers dare.
Pathways lit by fervent sparks,
Whispered secrets in the dark.

Through storms of doubt, it flies anew,
A spirit born from every hue.
Glowing reverberations rise,
Igniting hope beneath the skies.

When shadows threaten to consume,
The firebird breaks forth from gloom.
With every flap, a brand new way,
Guiding hearts to brighter day.

Shimmering Reflections of the Rising Flame

Dancing embers, warm embrace,
Flickering soft, a sacred space.
In the twilight, stories weave,
Shimmering hopes that we believe.

Reflections cast in golden light,
Whispers carried by the night.
Every spark a memory bright,
Guiding paths with pure delight.

As flames engulf the waning day,
Shadows play and gently sway.
In the heat, our dreams ignite,
A canvas painted with our might.

The rising flame, a sight to behold,
A beacon strong, defiant, bold.
With each flicker, strength does blend,
Where past and present gently mend.

Onward through the dusky veil,
Together we shall never fail.
Shimmering reflections call our name,
In unity, we feed the flame.

Brilliance in the Wake of Wings

In the dawn, a burst of light,
Brilliance dances, spirits bright.
Wings unfurl, a graceful rise,
Chasing dreams across the skies.

Nature's canvas brushed with cheer,
Echoes of the world so dear.
Through azure realms where whispers play,
We find our truth along the way.

Every feather tells a tale,
Of journeys grand, where hopes prevail.
In the wake of wings, we soar,
Brilliance shines forevermore.

In the breezes, soft and sweet,
Life's adventures we repeat.
With hearts full of wonder bright,
Chasing beauty, born of light.

With each flap, the world unfolds,
Stories waiting to be told.
In the dance of skyward grace,
We find our home, our rightful place.

Echoes of Splendor from the Ashes

In the quiet, whispers rise,
Memories dance beneath the skies.
From the embers, beauty gleams,
In shadows, the light still beams.

Fragments of dreams take flight,
Casting colors in the night.
What was lost now finds its way,
In the dawn of a new day.

Hope ignites the flickering flame,
For every heart that feels the same.
From the ruins, new paths emerge,
With every pulse, the spirits surge.

In the garden where sorrow weeps,
The soil nourished, promise keeps.
From ashes, blossoms draw their breath,
Life anew, transcending death.

Together, we rise from despair,
Hands united, souls laid bare.
In the echoes of what has passed,
A legacy of love amassed.

Gleaming Wings Under a Starry Veil

In the stillness of the night,
Wings unfurl, taking flight.
Stars above whisper and sway,
Guiding hearts on their way.

Beneath the heavens, secrets lie,
Dreams awaken, hopes will fly.
With every shimmer, worlds align,
In a dance divine, intertwine.

Gleaming colors streak the sky,
As the moonlight breathes a sigh.
Every wish, a thread of gold,
A story waiting to be told.

Through the darkness, softly glows,
A tapestry of love that flows.
Underneath a cosmic spell,
We find a place where spirits dwell.

Soaring high on currents bright,
We embrace the endless night.
In these moments, pure and rare,
Together, free, beyond compare.

The Incandescent Call of Rebirth

From the depths of silent night,
A spark ignites, illuminating light.
Whispers echo, calling near,
A symphony that all can hear.

Every heartbeat, every sigh,
Marks the journey as we fly.
Crimson dawn breaks through the past,
In its glow, we are steadfast.

The river flows, a timeless creed,
Carving paths where hope is freed.
Upon the canvas, colors blend,
In every stroke, we find our friend.

With each breath, renewal breathes,
In the tapestry, woven leaves.
A world reborn, with every tear,
The incandescent call draws near.

Expectant hands reach for the sky,
Gathering dreams that will not die.
In the circle, life asserts,
From the ashes, beauty spurts.

Vibrations in the Glow of Transformation

Beneath the surface, beats the pulse,
Awakening life in gentle waltz.
The tides of change begin to rise,
Underneath the shifting skies.

Every ripple, a story told,
Of journeys brave, of hearts bold.
In the glow, the colors swirl,
As the universe begins to twirl.

In quiet moments, echoes bloom,
Transforming shadows into room.
From darkness, light finds its place,
Vibrations dance with endless grace.

Connected threads weave through the night,
With every heartbeat, we ignite.
In the symphony, we sway and hum,
To the rhythm of what's yet to come.

Through the fog, a vision clear,
We rise anew, devoid of fear.
In the glow of all that's true,
Transformation calls to me and you.

The Horizon of Fiery Possibilities

In the glimmer of dawn's embrace,
New dreams awaken, take their place.
Golden rays dance on the sea,
Whispers of what could be.

Boundless visions in the sky,
With every heartbeat, we will fly.
Tales of adventure spark the air,
Unwritten paths ignite our dare.

Beyond the mountains, the flames are bright,
Radiant hues paint the night.
Step by step, our futures call,
Together we will rise or fall.

With every challenge, we grow bold,
In the furnace of fate, our hearts unfold.
The horizon beckons, vast and wide,
With fiery possibilities as our guide.

Together we'll chase the fleeting hour,
Kindled spirits, we shall empower.
In the glow of dreams, in every sight,
We forge our truth, our endless light.

A Lamentation in Fiery Tones

Cold shadows dance in the fading light,
Echoing whispers of lost delight.
In the heart, the embers burn,
For the passions that we yearn.

Silent cries in the ember's glow,
Thoughts of what we'll never know.
Winds of change, cruel and swift,
Stealing dreams, the heart's rift.

Shattered hopes on the ground lie,
As memories fade, and we sigh.
Each heartbeat a reminder of pain,
In the ashes, we find our gain.

Yet through the sorrow, a spark remains,
A flicker of hope, though it wanes.
With every tear that we shed,
In fiery tones, our souls are fed.

From the ruins, we shall arise,
In the twilight's grace, our spirits fly.
Though we mourn, our hearts will learn,
From the lamentation, we shall return.

Dreams of Flame in Twilight's Embers

Twilight descends with a gentle sigh,
Painting the canvas of the sky.
In the quiet, dreams ignite,
Whispers of flame in the night.

Stars awaken, bright and bold,
Stories of longing yet untold.
In the depth of darkness, we see
Flickering visions of what could be.

The embers dance in the cool breeze,
Carrying secrets among the trees.
With every shadow, hopes arise,
In the heart of night, laughter flies.

Each dream a treasure, fiercely held,
A passion within, vividly compelled.
Through the twilight, we roam as one,
To the rhythm of the rising sun.

With every heartbeat, the flames will burn,
Lessons learned and hearts that yearn.
In dreams of fire, we'll forever stay,
Illuminated paths, our guiding way.

Wings of Hope in the Ascent

Upward we soar, on whispers of air,
Carried by dreams, free from despair.
With open hearts, we spread our wings,
Embracing the hope that the future brings.

Each challenge faced, a mountain climbed,
In the journey, our spirits rhymed.
Holding fast to visions bright,
In the dance of shadows and light.

In the ascent, we find our grace,
With every moment, we embrace.
Through trials faced, we will not bend,
A testament of strength we'll send.

The winds of change may push and pull,
Yet in our hearts, a fire full.
With wings of hope, we rise above,
Soaring high on currents of love.

With courage stitched in every seam,
We chase the echoes of our dream.
In the journey, we find our way,
Hope's ascent, our grand ballet.

Illuminated Songs of the Eternal Flame

Flickering whispers paint the night,
Echoes of warmth in the pale moonlight.
Hearts aligned with the embers' glow,
Songs of the eternal, soft and slow.

Longing and hope entwined in air,
Fingers stretch, surrendering care.
Beneath the stars, we lose our fears,
Voices rise, dissolving our tears.

In the silence, flames softly hum,
Promises made, forever to come.
Every heartbeat aligned with the spark,
A journey begins, igniting the dark.

Light of the moment, so vivid, so bright,
Guiding the lost, a beacon of light.
We dance in circles, swaying with grace,
Each flicker, a story, a sacred space.

Together we sing, a chorus of joy,
As shadows wane, new dreams we employ.
In the warmth of the fire, we find our way,
Bathed in the glow of a new born day.

Glistening Shadows Cast by the Fire's Dance

The fire sways, a living brush,
Painting shadows in a gentle hush.
Whispers of night in its embrace,
Each flicker tells of time and space.

Dancing lightly, the flames unite,
Casting stories in golden light.
Twinkles gleam where the shadows play,
As dreams unfurl, night turns to day.

Echoes shimmer, hearts entwined,
In the glow of embers, we find.
Every movement, a tale unfolds,
In glistening shadows, the fire molds.

We gather close, warmth all around,
In whispered secrets, love is found.
Kindled spirits rise and fly,
Under the watchful, starlit sky.

So let us linger, here and now,
Under the dance, take a bow.
In the sacred glow, we embrace the chance,
Glistening shadows, moving in dance.

Celestial Radiance of the Reborn

From ashes, rise with radiant grace,
Stars align in the cosmic space.
Awakening souls, a brilliant sight,
Celestial beings, igniting the night.

Each breath, a spark of life anew,
In the universe, endless and true.
Galaxies whisper, in harmony, sing,
Reviving the hope that each heart can bring.

Celestial radiance, pure and clear,
Transcending fear, we hold it dear.
In the silence, the cosmos swells,
A symphony of love that forever dwells.

Hearts unbroken, soaring high,
Caught in the web of the vast sky.
Together we journey, hand in hand,
In the sacred dance of the reborn land.

Under the starlight, we find our way,
In this divine moment, we choose to stay.
With every heartbeat, we embrace the dawn,
As celestial whispers sing of the reborn.

Fire and Light: The Dance of Renewal

In the heart of night, fire ignites,
With every flicker, hope ignites.
Light and shadow, entwined in sway,
Dance of renewal, come what may.

From ashes to brilliance, we unfold,
A tale of courage, vibrant and bold.
In every spark, a story flows,
Of dreams reborn, as the river glows.

The warmth envelops, spirits rise,
In the dance, we find the skies.
Together we move, souls intertwined,
In the embrace of love, kindly aligned.

Fire and light, a magical trance,
Holding our hearts in this sacred dance.
Unveiling truths beneath the flame,
In every step, we acknowledge our name.

So let us gather, here in this place,
Embracing the fire's warm embrace.
Through light and shadow, we will journey on,
In the dance of renewal, where we belong.

Whispers of Radiance in Flight

Whispers rise with the dawn's light,
A symphony of dreams taking flight.
Tender hopes weave through the air,
Softly glimmering, beyond compare.

In the hush where shadows play,
Golden hues chase the night away.
Each flutter dances, each sigh sings,
A magic spun on ephemeral wings.

Nature's breath, a gentle caress,
Guides lost souls toward happiness.
In the twilight, secrets unfold,
Stories of warmth, quietly told.

Hearts embrace the sun-kissed morn,
Radiance woven, passion reborn.
With every whisper, the world ignites,
As dreams take shape in dazzling flights.

So let us soar on melodies bright,
In whispers of radiance, pure delight.
Through azure skies, we'll find our way,
In the dance of life, forever sway.

The Ember's Glimmering Path

An ember spark in twilight's glow,
Guiding journeys where few dare go.
A flicker on the darkest night,
Leading hearts to the dawn's first light.

With every step on this glowing trace,
Shadows retreat, leaving no space.
A warmth within the chill of fate,
Embers whisper to illuminate.

Through valleys deep and peaks so high,
The glimmering path will never die.
In every heart a fire resides,
As we travel where courage guides.

Embers dance in a cosmic waltz,
Celebrating life, without faults.
In the silence, we hear their call,
And rise together, never to fall.

The journey flows like a river's breath,
Echoing tales of life and death.
So let us walk this uncharted way,
In the ember's glow, we shall stay.

Reverberations of Celestial Fire

Stars ignite in the velvet sky,
Whispers of time in a cosmic sigh.
Celestial fire blazes bright,
A tapestry woven in endless night.

From distant realms, their voices ring,
Echoes of ancient, forgotten spring.
In every pulse, a story told,
Of love and loss, both bold and gold.

Galaxies spin in a celestial dance,
Each twinkle a wish, a fleeting chance.
Reverberations crash like waves,
Carving dreams in the hearts of knaves.

Through the silence, we hear the sound,
Of cosmic hearts forever unbound.
In vastness, we find our place,
In this fire, there's a warm embrace.

So let the stars guide our way,
In the reverberations, we sway.
For in their glow, we all aspire,
To become one with celestial fire.

Wings of Dawn's Prophecy

A gentle breeze on the horizon,
Wings spread wide, ancient and wise.
Dawn whispers secrets of the day,
Each color paints the skies in play.

The prophecy found in morning's grace,
Awakens dreams through time and space.
Fluttering softly on the edge of night,
Birds of omen in joyous flight.

With every beat, a promise soars,
Of love, of hope, and open doors.
The sunrise holds our whispered fears,
Transforming them to joyful tears.

In the glow of the amber hour,
We find our strength, our inner power.
Wings of dawn carry us far,
Guided by the light of the morning star.

So take a breath and spread your wings,
Embrace the gifts that the day brings.
In the dawn's embrace, we rise and see,
The prophecy of what we're meant to be.

Echoes from Ashes of Yesterday

In the quiet spaces of the night,
Whispers linger, shadows take flight.
Memories dance on the edge of time,
Carried softly in a haunting rhyme.

Fleeting moments, lost and found,
Resonate softly, a haunting sound.
Each echo tells of love once bright,
Now fading softly into the night.

Through the remnants of yesterday's glow,
Lessons learned in the undertow.
From ashes rise, a phoenix reborn,
In the heart of twilight, hope is worn.

Past and present, woven as one,
Stories entwined until the day is done.
In every echo, a truth resides,
Time's gentle hand, where memory guides.

So let the echoes softly sing,
Of all the joy and pain they bring.
For in each whisper, we find our way,
Through the echoes from ashes of yesterday.

Dancing Flames of Celebration

Underneath the starlit sky,
Flames leap up, reaching high.
Joy ignites in every heart,
As the night begins to start.

Laughter dances in the air,
Warming souls, banishing care.
In the flicker, dreams unite,
Sparks of hope, shivering light.

Voices rise in sweet refrain,
Melodies broken by the rain.
Yet through storms, we stand our ground,
In each heartbeat, love is found.

Crimson embers, glowing bright,
Guide us through the velvet night.
As we twirl, the world stands still,
In the flame's embrace, we feel the thrill.

Celebration in every sway,
Happiness will find its way.
Together in this night we stay,
In dancing flames, we drift away.

A Path of Radiance in the Sky

Above the clouds, a light unfolds,
A radiant path, a tale retold.
Colors blend in the azure sea,
As stars unveil their mystery.

Each twinkling note, a wish released,\nGuiding travelers,
never ceased.
In galaxies where wonders soar,
A journey starts, forevermore.

The moonlight bathes the land below,
Casting dreams in a silver glow.
With every step, our spirits rise,
On a path of radiance in the skies.

Hearts unite in silent prayer,
Grateful for the love we share.
Through the vastness, hand in hand,
We seek the light across the land.

So let us wander, brave and free,
Chasing horizons, you and me.
On this destined quest we trod,
Finding solace in the sky, our abode.

The Fire's Silent Cry for Wings

In the hearth where embers gleam,
A whispered wish, a secret dream.
The fire burns with a longing sigh,
Yearning deep for wings to fly.

Crimson flames, they leap and dance,
Caught in a wild, entrancing trance.
Each flicker holds a tale untold,
Of journeys waiting to unfold.

As wood gives in to heat and ash,
The spirit yearns for freedom's flash.
In every spark, a heartbeat flows,
A silent cry only the fire knows.

Amidst the warmth, a gusting breeze,
Carries whispers through the trees.
The fire dreams of distant lands,
Where it may soar, where it understands.

And in the night, beneath the stars,
The fire's heart breaks through its bars.
For every flame desires to sing,
The fire's silent cry for wings.

Beckoning Flare of Forgotten Times

In shadows cast by fading light,
The whispers tell of distant night.
A flame ignites the embers' dance,
Recalling dreams of lost romance.

The echoes linger, soft and sweet,
With every heartbeat, memories greet.
A glow that once lit paths unknown,
Now marks the space we call our own.

Each flicker speaks of days gone by,
Of laughter shared, a fleeting sigh.
In twilight's arms, we find our grace,
A flame that time cannot erase.

Yet as the dark begins to creep,
The flare invites us deep to leap.
To journey forth, reclaim the past,
And in that light, our souls held fast.

In every spark, the stories glow,
Of battles fought and love's sweet woe.
The beckoning flare, a guiding star,
Illuminates where memories are.

The Chorus of Phoenix Flames

In hues of red and gold, they rise,
The joyous heart beneath the skies.
A symphony of light ignites,
As ashes whisper of new flights.

With every note, a spirit sings,
A melody that boldly clings.
The phoenix flames, a dance of fate,
In the warmth, we celebrate.

O soaring hearts that seek to shine,
Within the fire, a spark divine.
The chorus calls, let shadows flee,
Rebirth awaits, we are set free.

In twilight's grace, the flames will swirl,
Each ember holds a vibrant world.
Together bound, we take our claim,
For life anew, we fan the flame.

So sing the songs of rising dreams,
In every blaze, the fire redeems.
The chorus of the phoenix bright,
In unity, we find our light.

Wings Embraced in Twilight's Glow

As dusk unfolds, the sky ignites,
With colors bold, our hearts take flight.
The wings we spread, in hush we soar,
Embraced by twilight, evermore.

The whispers float on gentle breeze,
In every rustle through the trees.
Together, we chase fading light,
With dreams entwined, we rise from night.

In shadows danced, our spirits weave,
A tapestry of what we believe.
In twilight's glow, we find our way,
Where night and day in union sway.

The stars emerge, a guiding spark,
As wings unfold against the dark.
We chase the echoes, find our strength,
In twilight's embrace, we grow at length.

So let us fly, our hearts aglow,
In every moment, let dreams flow.
With wings embraced in twilight's song,
We carve our path, where we belong.

The Elysian Flare of New Beginnings

From realms unknown, the light descends,
A beacon bright, where hope transcends.
The flare ignites, a path so clear,
In Elysium, we conquer fear.

With every dawn, the world reborn,
The whispers shared, no longer torn.
The beauty found in every phase,
Illuminates our hopeful gaze.

In gardens lush, we plant our dreams,
With open hearts, the sunlight beams.
The promise blooms in vibrant hues,
As life unfolds, new shades infused.

So let us walk, hand in hand,
Through realms of joy, a golden land.
The flare of life, forever bright,
In Elysian grace, we find our light.

With every spark that lights the way,
We cherish now, and greet the day.
For here we stand, in love's embrace,
New beginnings spark in every place.

The Resplendent Flicker Through Time

In shadows cast by ancient trees,
A flicker whispers through the leaves,
Echoes of a distant chime,
Carrying secrets held by time.

With every breeze, a tale unfolds,
Of dreams and hopes, and stories told,
Illuminating paths once trod,
In the quiet touch of God.

Through golden rays that softly spill,
Life dances on with brilliant thrill,
A tapestry of light and sound,
In every pulse, a heartbeat found.

Stars emerge as night descends,
Their light a guide, a faithful trend,
Whispering wishes to the sky,
In resplendent flickers, we fly.

So hold this light within your heart,
Know every end is a new start,
For in the depths of time's embrace,
We find love's ever-constant grace.

Feathered Flames and Burning Wishes

From embered dreams, the spirits rise,
With feathered flames that paint the skies,
They twist and turn in swirling flight,
Igniting hearts with pure delight.

Every wish born from the fire,
Transforms the soul, ignites desire,
As hopes take wing, they soar and glide,
In the warmth of passions untried.

With every flutter, moments gleam,
Holding the thrill of deepest dream,
A serenade of soft embrace,
In feathered trails, we find our place.

Let go your worries, breathe anew,
For burning wishes lift us through,
In the dance of flames, we find our way,
Through twilight's glow to break of day.

Embrace the heat, let courage bloom,
In the flickering light, dispel the gloom,
For every wish, like flames, can soar,
In feathered flames, we live for more.

Glows of Rebirth on Ascending Wings

In dawn's embrace, new life awakens,
With glows of rebirth, the heart forsakens,
The shadows of past, long held tight,
To rise anew in radiant light.

On ascending wings, our spirits soar,
Breaking the bounds, we yearn for more,
With every flap, the world unfolds,
As stories of courage and hope are told.

A symphony of colors burst,
In whispered dreams, we quench our thirst,
For in each glow, a promise lies,
Of endless love that never dies.

Through every challenge, every fall,
We rise again, we heed the call,
To dance with joy, as hearts ignite,
In glows of rebirth, we find our flight.

So lift your gaze, embrace the dawn,
For every end is just a pawn,
In life's grand game, we take our try,
With ascending wings, we touch the sky.

The Intermingling of Fire and Hope

In a world where shadows blend,
Fire and hope begin to mend,
Each flicker held within the dark,
A promise strong, a vital spark.

With every flame that burns so bright,
Hope dances close, defying night,
Interwoven dreams, they intertwine,
In a tapestry of fate divine.

Through the ashes, new life springs,
In the embrace of fiery wings,
We rise from loss, we bloom anew,
With hope aglow, our spirits true.

Let hearts unite in this embrace,
For every fire finds its place,
In the struggle that we face each day,
Together, we'll light the way.

So gather 'round this mystic blaze,
And let our souls ignite with praise,
For in the warmth of love entwined,
We'll find the strength to not be blind.

Songs of the Eternal Feather

In whispers of dawn, the feathers fly,
Carried by winds that softly sigh.
They dance with grace, a timeless theme,
Echoes of dreams in a gentle beam.

Through forests deep, their stories call,
Creating bridges, uniting us all.
Each hue a note in a grand old song,
Binding the worlds where we all belong.

A tapestry woven with threads of light,
Guiding our hearts through the night.
In the stillness, the feathers gleam,
Whispering secrets, living the dream.

From peaks of the mountains to valleys low,
The songs of the winged ones ever flow.
In harmony's grasp, we find our place,
Embraced by the beauty of feathered grace.

The Uprising of Starlit Ashes

From embers cold, the starlight glows,
Through shadows deep, a power grows.
Whispers of hope in the midnight air,
A dance of dreams, beyond despair.

The ashes rise in a swirling spree,
Rebuilding worlds where we long to be.
In cosmic winds, they twirl and sway,
Guiding lost souls to a brighter day.

With every spark, a fury burns,
In silence born, the heart still yearns.
The starlit ashes, a fierce embrace,
Awakening spirits to time and space.

Gather around, let voices soar,
In unity's song, we'll fight for more.
Together we'll face the gray and dim,
In the uprising, our hope begins.

Vibrations of Celestial Renewal

Awake, dear heart, to the ancient sound,
In cosmic waves, true love is found.
Each note a promise of life reborn,
In the cycle of night, and the blush of morn.

The universe hums its sacred tune,
In every star and crescent moon.
Feel the vibrations, let them unwind,
Revel in rhythms that bind humankind.

Through valleys low and mountains high,
The song of renewal fills the sky.
With each pulse, a spirit wakes,
Breath of creation, as the stillness breaks.

Join in the chorus, let voices blend,
In waves of harmony, let hearts mend.
Together we stand, a luminous band,
Resonating with the universe, hand in hand.

The Resurgent Flame's Serenade

From ashes deep, the flame ascends,
A serenade where the darkness ends.
With flickering light, the shadows flee,
In the heart's embrace, we learn to be.

Listen closely to the fire's song,
A tale of strength where we belong.
With every spark, our spirits rise,
Casting away the night's disguise.

In fields of gold where embers play,
The resurgent flame ignites the day.
In unity's flame, let courage swell,
Together we thrive, together we dwell.

For in the warmth of the blazing light,
We find our paths, we claim our right.
The serenade sings of love and grace,
In the flame's glow, we embrace.

Sparks of Brilliance in Twilight's Embrace

In the whisper of dusk, dreams take flight,
Glistening softly, stars ignite.
A canvas of shadows, painted in gold,
Stories of wonder, quietly unfold.

Crimson and violet dance in the air,
Nature's soft lullaby, beyond compare.
Each flicker of light, a heartbeat of night,
Guiding the lost with their tender sight.

Mountains hold secrets beneath the deep sky,
Echoes of magic that never say die.
In twilight's embrace, we find our way,
Chasing the dreams that refuse to stay.

Glimmers of hope, like whispers of fate,
Shine through the shadows, shall not wait.
In silence they promise, love's warm caress,
Brilliance unbridled, through time we'll possess.

Together we dance, in a world set apart,
Forever entwined, as we share one heart.
Sparks of brilliance, in twilight's sweet grace,
In shadows of night, we find our place.

Ethereal Twinkles in a Fiery Horizon

The horizon ablaze, with colors so bright,
Dancing like flames against the dark night.
Each twinkle a promise, in vastness they soar,
Embers of dreams, forever explore.

Fiery horizons, where day meets the stars,
Awakening spirit, beyond earthly bars.
In whispers of twilight, the universe sings,
The magic of longing, on luminous wings.

A tapestry woven, with threads made of light,
Framing each heartbeat, igniting the night.
Ethereal beauty, in nature's embrace,
Sparkling with joy, as shadows give chase.

On the edge of the world, where legends reside,
Boundless horizons, with nothing to hide.
Each flicker and glimmer, a song to behold,
Tales of the radiant, in twilight retold.

As daylight retreats, embracing the dark,
The fiery horizon ignites a bright spark.
Ethereal twinkles, in the sky's deep embrace,
Unfolding the mysteries of time and space.

Winged Light: A Song of Resurrection

From ashes we rise, with wings made of flame,
Unfurling our spirits, no longer the same.
A hymn of revival, sweet echoes we sing,
In the dance of rebirth, hope takes to wing.

In the cradle of night, the stars intertwine,
Reclaiming our power, our souls now divine.
With each gentle whisper, the dawn breaks anew,
Winged light ascends, painting skies blue.

The shadows retreat, where courage burned bright,
Shattering silence with radiant light.
A melody woven through heartbeats and sighs,
Carried on wings, as we learn to arise.

Resilient and strong, we embrace every scar,
Each challenge encountered, our guiding star.
In moments of darkness, we gather our might,
Song of resurrection, we choose to ignite.

With wings full of freedom, we soar to the skies,
Awakening dreams that we dared to despise.
Winged light surrounds us, a journey begun,
A song of rebirth, forever we run.

Enkindled Spirits in the Celestial Sea

In the celestial sea, we float and we dream,
Enkindled by starlight, a radiant beam.
The whispers of cosmos, a shimmering guide,
Carrying stories where wonder can hide.

Together we sail on waves of pure light,
Drifting through galaxies, lost in delight.
Each heartbeat a rhythm, a cosmic refrain,
Exploring eternity, free from the chain.

Galactic enchantment, where shadows dissolve,
In embrace of the night, our spirits evolve.
We dance with the comets, the meteors fall,
In the vastness of space, we answer the call.

With each cosmic glance, we ignite the unknown,
Tracing the nebulae, together we've grown.
Enkindled spirits, in this boundless expanse,
In the dance of creation, we find our romance.

Under celestial tides, our hearts intertwine,
Exploring the universe, our dreams align.
In this sea of starlight, forever we'll be,
Enkindled spirits, in the celestial sea.

A Tapestry of Celestial Embers

Stars weave tales in the night,
Whispers of dreams take flight.
Threads of light entwined so bright,
A cosmic dance, pure delight.

Galaxies swirl with grace,
Infinite wonder fills space.
Time and light embrace in chase,
In this celestial place.

Nebulas paint the skies bold,
Stories of ages untold.
Where shadows and light behold,
Mysteries in stardust rolled.

Comets race with fiery trails,
Echo of ancient tales.
In each sparkle, love prevails,
As the universe exhales.

In silence, the night unfolds,
Cradling hearts in its holds.
In the dark, visions behold,
A tapestry of dreams foretold.

When Ashes Whisper Sweet Secrets

Embers whisper in the dark,
Echoing memories, a spark.
Softly crumbling, life's arc,
From ashes, hearts leave their mark.

Scattered remnants of the past,
Moments fleeting, yet they last.
In the silence, shadows cast,
In the warmth, connections vast.

When the night begins to wane,
Amongst the whispers, joy and pain.
Tales of love, loss, and gain,
In the stillness, hearts remain.

Through the smoke, ghosts arise,
Revealing truth behind the lies.
Secrets woven, wise and wise,
In the ashes, hope complies.

With each flicker, a choice made,
In the shadows, dreams conveyed.
From the embers, light cascades,
In soft whispers, love is laid.

The Incandescence of Reborn Dreams

In the cradle of night, hope breathes,
Fragrance of wishes among the leaves.
Stars illuminate paths to seize,
As passion ignites, the heart believes.

With each dawn, light pours anew,
Casting shadows, revealing the true.
In the brilliance, joy breaks through,
Reborn dreams embrace the view.

Through the challenges faced in time,
The spirit rises, a silent chime.
With every struggle, every climb,
Dreams resurface, pure as rhyme.

Glimmers of love in every heart,
A tapestry woven, never apart.
In the glow, we all play our part,
Igniting the world, a work of art.

Through the cycles, the dance persists,
In the echoes of life's twists.
In the light, we create, exist,
The incandescence of dreamers kissed.

Wings Flapping to the Rhythm of Fire

In the dawn, flames start to rise,
Wings unfurl beneath the skies.
With each beat, ambition flies,
Chasing dreams where passion lies.

Fires crackle, whispers reign,
Encouragement wrapped in pain.
In the heat, we break the chain,
The rhythm sings, none remain.

Through the air, warmth ignites,
Fueling hearts with daring fights.
With each flap, the spirit lights,
Guided by dreams and starry nights.

Across the skies, the embers trail,
Echoes of the heart's own sail.
In the blaze, we will not fail,
Through the storm, we shall prevail.

As the sun sets, wings still soar,
In the glow, we hear the roar.
With every heartbeat, we explore,
To the rhythm of fire, forevermore.

Radiance on the Edge of Twilight

The sun dips low, brushed in hues,
Whispers of gold, the sky imbues.
Shadows stretch, fading in grace,
A moment held in time and space.

Night creatures stir, the silence sings,
Softly wrapped in twilight's wings.
Stars flicker with a distant glow,
Echoes of light where dreams may flow.

Beneath the veil, the world holds deep,
Secrets of time that we could keep.
As darkness drapes the evening sky,
Radiant thoughts begin to fly.

A palette twirls, the colors blend,
Nature's masterpiece knows no end.
In every fade, a promise new,
Twilight whispers, "I'll shine for you."

So let the twilight guide your way,
In fading light, we find our stay.
Each moment crafted in this art,
Radiance shines within the heart.

Inner Fire and Outer Radiance

Within the soul, a flame awakens,
A battle fought, yet never shaken.
Kindling spark in the silent night,
Igniting dreams with fervent light.

Outer glow reflects the inner,
In the quiet, we find the winner.
Hearts entwined with passion's trace,
We blaze a path, a warm embrace.

Fires of hope burn ever bright,
Guiding us through the shadowed night.
In every breath, our forces blend,
Inner strength, our steadfast friend.

Resilience fuels the beating heart,
Each flickering flame a work of art.
As embers dance in the air so free,
Our radiant spirits find harmony.

Together we forge through storms and fear,
With inner fire, our souls grow clear.
In the twilight, we bask in fate,
As outer radiance becomes our state.

A Symphony of Ashen Dreams

In the stillness, dreams take flight,
Softly drifting in the night.
Whispers left in shadows gleam,
Crafting tales of ash and dream.

A symphony of soul's delight,
Echoes linger, sweet and bright.
Fleeting moments, fragile dance,
Painted visions in a trance.

Each fragment tells a story old,
Of ashes soft, of glories told.
In silence, we hear the sighs,
Deep within where longing lies.

Melodies of heart and time,
Sculpting landscapes rich in rhyme.
In every note, a wish is spun,
A world reborn, when day is done.

Let the ashes whisper low,
In dreams we weave, we ebb and flow.
Through the night, till dawn redeems,
We sing together, ash and dreams.

The Celestial Dance of Light and Flame

Beneath the stars, light takes its stand,
Shadows twirl in a cosmic band.
Flame and glow, a dance so grand,
As darkness yields to a guiding hand.

Celestial bodies waltz in time,
Bright as dreams in vibrant rhyme.
Whispers blend in twilight's shade,
As beauty's tapestry is laid.

Stars ignite with a fervent spark,
Illuminating the quiet dark.
In every twinkle, hope's embraced,
A universe of love interlaced.

Galaxies swirl in elegant flight,
Spiraling jewels in the deep night.
Each moment glows with life's embrace,
The dance of light in sacred space.

So let your spirit rise and soar,
In the celestial rhythm, forevermore.
With every heartbeat, feel the claim,
In the vastness, we thrive in flame.

The Dance of Kindled Spirits

In twilight's glow, they sway and twirl,
With laughter bright, a joyous whirl.
Their gentle grace, a sight divine,
The kindled spirits, brightly shine.

They weave through dreams, like whispers soft,
In every heart, their warmth aloft.
With every step, a bond deepens,
In love and light, their dance strengthens.

Around the fire, stories unfold,
Of timeless joys and truths retold.
In every eye, a spark ignites,
A dance of souls, on starry nights.

Together they rise, in radiant flight,
Their spirits free, in pure delight.
In harmony, they paint the sky,
With colors bright that never die.

The dance goes on, through space and time,
A melody sweet, a rhythm sublime.
In every heartbeat, they remain,
The kindled spirits, free from pain.

Retracing Hues of the Phoenix

From ashes born, the phoenix soars,
With fiery wings, it seeks new shores.
In radiant hues, it paints the dawn,
A tale of hope, forever drawn.

Each feather shines, a vibrant tale,
Of trials faced, where others fail.
Through storms it braves, with steadfast might,
Retracing paths to endless light.

In shades of crimson, golden blaze,
A journey long, through life's maze.
With every rise, the past laid bare,
A reminder of the beauty shared.

Emerging strong from every fall,
The phoenix answers its own call.
With every hue, its spirit gleams,
Resilience found in every dream.

As shadows fade, the colors blend,
A dance of life that won't soon end.
The phoenix flies, both bold and free,
Retracing hues of destiny.

Shimmering Night's Feathered Resurrection

Under the stars, a whisper glows,
The night unfolds, as silence grows.
With feathered grace, the shadows play,
In shimmering light, they find their way.

A dance of dreams, in moonlit skies,
Where spirits rise, and hope defies.
Each shimmer holds a story's breath,
A resurrection teased from death.

In velvet dark, the night is deep,
As shadows waltz while dreamers sleep.
With every flicker, a spark is born,
A tale of light, a new dawn sworn.

Through endless night, they flutter bright,
The feathered ones, a beautiful sight.
In every heart, their music hums,
A song of life, as daylight comes.

As dawn approaches, night takes flight,
With whispered vows that end the night.
The feathered dance, an echo's grace,
A shimmering night, a sacred space.

The Awakening Flicker of Dusk

As daylight wanes, the shadows fall,
An awakening flicker, a soft call.
In hues of orange, red, and gold,
A whisper of secrets, yet untold.

Through branches sways, the evening breeze,
A gentle stir, amidst the trees.
With every rustle, a story shared,
Of hopes reborn, of dreams declared.

The stars emerge, like diamonds cast,
The dusk unveils the beauty vast.
In twilight's arms, the world will pause,
In every flicker, a breath, a cause.

As night approaches, the calm sets in,
A flicker of light, where shadows begin.
Each heartbeat echoes, the dusk weaves tight,
A tapestry rich, of day and night.

With every flicker, a promise made,
A dance of dusk, never to fade.
In twilight's glow, the heart finds peace,
An awakening flicker, a sweet release.

Illuminated Whispers of the Abyss

In shadows deep, the secrets weave,
A tapestry of dreams that cleave.
Whispers echo through the night,
Brightly glowing, shunning fright.

Stars emerge from waters dark,
Guiding souls, igniting spark.
Each ripple tells a timeless tale,
Of hidden paths and ships that sail.

Beneath the waves, the spirits glide,
In silence vast, where shadows bide.
With every breath, a haunting song,
The abyss whispers, deep and strong.

Reflections dance on liquid skin,
Where light and dark entwine within.
A realm forgotten, yet so near,
In the depths, we face our fear.

Illuminated dreams arise,
Carried softly, starry skies.
Through the depths, we journey far,
In whispers, find our guiding star.

When Fire Meets the Horizon

As daylight fades and embers glow,
The battlefield of dusk unfolds slow.
A fiery kiss on the silent sea,
A tapestry of warmth, wild and free.

The evening's breath ignites the skies,
In every hue, dreamers rise.
With passion strong, the flames take flight,
Embracing dusk, surrendering night.

Crimson and gold get intertwined,
Unraveling peace where hearts have pined.
The horizon whispers secrets bold,
Of stories shared and memories told.

In the distance, shadows chase,
Every flicker, a warm embrace.
The world transforms in glowing rays,
In the dance of light, hope stays.

From embers sparks of dreams ignite,
In the heart of darkness shines the light.
When fire meets the edge of day,
New beginnings gently sway.

A Celestial Call to Wings

The night unfurls its velvet cloak,
With stardust dreams and moonlight spoke.
In whispered winds, the skies awake,
A call to wings, a chance to take.

Awash in color, galaxies spin,
Inviting souls to dance within.
Each flicker bright, a promise made,
To soar above, unafraid, unflayed.

With open hearts and restless minds,
We chase the shadows fate unwinds.
To touch the stars, to break the chains,
And write our names where wonder reigns.

In every heartbeat, echoes swell,
A celestial hymn, a magic spell.
The universe bows, inviting flight,
As we ascend to greet the night.

With newfound strength and wings unfurled,
We traverse dreams, explore the world.
In unity, our spirits sing,
A symphony of hope takes wing.

Glinting Memories of the Phoenix

From ashes deep, a fire to rise,
A tale reborn beneath the skies.
With each rebirth, the memories gleam,
In glinting light, we find our dream.

The flame ignites with colors bright,
Painting shadows, erasing night.
With wings of gold, the phoenix flies,
Crafting legends, writing ties.

Through trials faced, the ember glows,
In every scar, a story sows.
A dance of strength through time and space,
In every heartbeat, we find grace.

So let the fire burn within,
In every loss, a chance to win.
With every flight, we leave a mark,
A legacy ignited from the dark.

In glinting memories, hopes reside,
Embracing change, the soul's true pride.
From ashes spring new tales to tell,
In phoenix flames, we rise and swell.

Wings of Light in the Gathering Dark

In twilight's embrace, shadows creep,
A whisper of hope, secrets we keep.
The stars start to shimmer, a delicate spark,
Illuminating dreams in the gathering dark.

Through the silence, a soft song calls,
Gently lifting the heart as it falls.
With wings of light, we dare to soar,
Over the depths, to a distant shore.

Each heartbeat a promise, each breath a prayer,
In the stillness, we find what is rare.
Together we rise, hand in hand,
In the glow of the night, we shall stand.

As shadows retreat, dawn's warmth descends,
The magic of night, the light it lends.
In unity, under the vast, endless sky,
We spread our wings, learning to fly.

With visions of future and echoes of past,
In the dance of the light, we are free at last.
The gathering dark can no longer confine,
For hope is our guide, in the stars we shine.

The Dream of Burning Skies

Beneath the canvas of crimson and gold,
A dream awakes, with stories untold.
The sun dips low, igniting the night,
In this symphony, we find our light.

Clouds painted boldly, in shades of desire,
Each breath fuels the relentless fire.
With every flicker, a tale to weave,
The heart knows not how to deceive.

As the world spins on, whispers elate,
In harmony, we dance, embracing our fate.
The dream of the skies, so daring, so bright,
Guiding lost souls through the heart of the night.

From ashes we rise, like phoenixes born,
In the warmth of the dusk, we are never forlorn.
Each ember a wish, each spark a chance,
In the dream of burning skies, we advance.

Here in the glow of a fading sun,
The journey is endless, never to shun.
With passion ignited, hearts intertwine,
Together we shine, through the night we align.

Echoes of Resurrection's Glow

From ashes we rise, in twilight's breath,
Embracing the beauty found in death.
Each heartbeat a whisper, each tear a song,
In echoes of light, we forge ourselves strong.

The dawn breaks softly, a promise reborn,
In the stillness, we mourn and adorn.
With colors of life, we paint the air,
Reviving the dreams that once lay bare.

In shadows that linger, a flicker ignites,
The hope of tomorrow, in long, quiet nights.
With courage, we step into the glow,
Carrying the light of what we once know.

The past whispers secrets, its echoes remain,
In the heart of the storm, we embrace the pain.
With each strand of light, a new path unfolds,
In the dance of resurrection, the future holds.

Together we rise, as one, we ascend,
In the brilliance of life, our hearts mend.
With echoes of love, we shall prevail,
In the glow of rebirth, we find our sail.

Fires of the Forgotten Horizon

Beyond the edges, where dreams take flight,
Fires beckon softly, throughout the night.
In fragrant whispers, the flames will call,
To the hearts of the weary, the lost, and the small.

As shadows entwine, with flickering light,
We gather our stories, igniting the night.
Each spark a memory, each blaze a tale,
Of journeys uncharted, destinies frail.

Through the haze of uncertainty, we shall roam,
Searching for solace, a place to call home.
In the warmth of the fire, together we sing,
Of the hope that the dawn of tomorrow will bring.

With courage, we face the vast unknown,
In the heart of the darkness, we gather, we've grown.
Fires of the horizon guide our way true,
In unity of spirit, we'll rise anew.

As dawn breaks the silence, a new day will dawn,
With embers of dreams, we'll carry on.
Through the fires of time, our souls intertwine,
In the tapestry of life, together, we shine.

A Brilliant Dance of Ember Trails

In twilight's grip, the embers sway,
The shadows pirouette, then play.
Flickers bright in the evening's hush,
Whispers of gold in a gentle rush.

Each spark a story, wild and free,
Tracing paths through the grand, dark sea.
They dance on air with fiery grace,
A brilliant waltz in time and space.

Embers rise, swirling in the night,
Lighting dreams, igniting flight.
In every flicker, a pulse divine,
A fleeting moment, eternity's sign.

Beneath the moon, their glow expands,
With fiery hands, they shape the sands.
A fleeting glimpse of a burning heart,
In the cosmic stage, they play their part.

As the night wanes, and shadows fade,
The dance of embers, a serenade.
With every flicker, a tale unfolds,
In brilliance born of ash and gold.

The Firebrand of Celestial Horizons

Above the world, the firebrand soars,
Brushing past the dreams' locked doors.
Its golden tail writes constellations,
Fueling the heart's deep fascination.

In the cradle of night, it weaves,
Through starry whispers, it believes.
Each spark ignites a cosmic sigh,
Under the watchful, endless sky.

Flames as fierce as the dawn's first light,
Chasing shadows with pure delight.
Across horizons, it boldly streams,
A blaze of wonder, born from dreams.

With every flicker, a wish takes flight,
Shattering silence, claiming the night.
A bridge between the earth and stars,
The firebrand sings of who we are.

As echoes fade in the dawn's embrace,
It leaves behind a fleeting trace.
A memory born from celestial strife,
The firebrand's dance, the pulse of life.

Echoing Whispers of the Burning Sky

In twilight skies where embers gleam,
Echoes whisper, soft as a dream.
Burning colors, alive and bright,
Fading gently into the night.

Rustling leaves sing tales of old,
Stories of warmth and flames so bold.
Voices rise, a choir of fire,
Crafting a song of pure desire.

Hints of crimson brush the clouds,
While shadows gather, thick as crowds.
In the stillness, the flames confide,
Secrets shared on the nighttime tide.

Every flicker carries a sound,
Whispers of love that still resound.
The burning sky holds memories dear,
In embers' glow, we draw them near.

As dusk settles, the echoes play,
Lighting the path as dreams display.
In the cool night air, a sacred sigh,
Through burning skies, our hopes will fly.

The Alchemy of Ashen Wings

From ashes rise, the wings take flight,
Crafted by fate in the still of night.
Glimmers of hope in a world of grey,
Transforming shadows, leading the way.

In flight's embrace, the past is shed,
Carried forth on whispers, led.
Alchemy of souls, the fires ignite,
Turning despair into purest light.

Each feather formed from embers bright,
An echo of dreams that took to light.
With every flap, the world awakes,
In the grace of change, the heart remakes.

Through storms they soar, unbound, unmatched,
In search of skies where dreams are hatched.
From ashes cold, a journey bold,
The wings of wonder, stories told.

As dawn approaches, the shadows fade,
Shimmering hope in the morning's jade.
With ethereal grace, they rise and sing,
The alchemy of life on ashen wings.

The Flight Towards Dazzling Hope

In the dawn's calm embrace, we arise,
Chasing dreams that dance in the skies.
Wings of courage lift us high,
Towards horizons where wishes lie.

Each heartbeat sounds like a call,
Guiding souls who rise and fall.
We soar on winds of fervent dreams,
Finding strength in whispered themes.

The sun spills gold on our flight,
A promise bright, a hopeful light.
Together we face the unknown,
Trusting the seeds of hope we've sown.

Through clouds we search for our way,
In every fear, we choose to stay.
With open hearts, we will ignite,
The path ahead, pure and bright.

So let us chase the gleaming star,
No distance too great, no dream too far.
For every flight holds the dawn's embrace,
In the dance of hope, we find our place.

Ashen Whispers of the Morning Light

Beneath the shroud of fading night,
Soft whispers stir with morning light.
The world awakens, slow, serene,
In ashen hues, a fleeting dream.

The stillness sings of hopes concealed,
In shadows deep, truth is revealed.
Each breath holds tales of the past,
While embers of dawn burn bright and vast.

Mist clings gently to the earth,
As memories find a new birth.
Awake, arise, the day draws near,
In its embrace, we cast our fear.

Soft sighs of dawn, like lovers' calls,
Wrap around the heart that falls.
In their arms, we find our peace,
And in this quiet, doubts release.

With every ray, the shadows part,
Revealing colors, touching hearts.
In ashen whispers, we take flight,
Embracing the warmth of morning light.

Chasing Shadows of Fiery Dawn

In the glow of the break of day,
We chase the shadows, come what may.
Fiery hues paint the waking sky,
As dreams stir softly, ready to fly.

Fingers stretch towards the glow,
Seeking warmth from the embers below.
Each moment flickers, alive with grace,
In this dance, we find our place.

The horizon blazes in vibrant red,
Whispering truths that were left unsaid.
Through the haze, our spirits roam,
Finding courage to call it home.

With fiery hearts, we break the chains,
Embracing the rush, ignoring the pains.
In shadows deep, new paths arise,
Bathed in light, beneath the skies.

Together we chase what lies ahead,
Filling our souls with words unsaid.
For in the dawn, we start anew,
Chasing shadows, vibrant and true.

Flames Beneath the Ascendant Breeze

Beneath the whispers of the trees,
We feel the flames in the gentle breeze.
Passion ignites in hearts that roam,
In wild adventures, we find our home.

The air is charged with sweet delight,
As dreams take flight in the soft twilight.
Each flicker calls out, a vibrant song,
Urging us forward, where we belong.

In every pulse, a fire ignites,
Guiding us through the darkest nights.
With hands entwined, we chase the spark,
Navigating through the shadows stark.

The world around us sways and bends,
As we write stories that never end.
With every breath, we dare to believe,
In the flames that flicker, we shall weave.

So let us rise with the new dawn's grace,
Embracing the fire in every space.
For life's a dance beneath the trees,
Flames of passion in the ascendant breeze.

Celestial Fire Meets Earthen Tides

In twilight's embrace, the stars ignite,
Ocean whispers secrets, soft and light.
Waves kiss the shore, where dreams abide,
Celestial fire meets earthen tides.

Sparks dance in the night, a gilded dance,
As the moon casts shadows, a fleeting glance.
Nature's own canvas, vast and wide,
Where celestial fire meets earthen tides.

Crimson and gold, the horizon blurs,
Time stands still as the world concurs.
In moments fleeting, we find our guide,
Celestial fire meets earthen tides.

Each flicker a tale, of love and strife,
Chasing the echoes of whispered life.
A cosmic embrace, our souls unite,
Celestial fire meets earthen tides.

Through night's quiet, a symphony plays,
The heartbeats of nature, in soft arrays.
In harmony's dance, we learn to glide,
Celestial fire meets earthen tides.

The Serene Embers of Forgotten Tales

In the hearth's glow, old stories breathe,
Silhouettes flicker, and shadows weave.
Whispers of yore in the amber flame,
The serene embers of forgotten tales.

Moonlight shimmers on a tapestry,
Each thread a path to a memory.
Lost voices echo, a ghostly frame,
The serene embers of forgotten tales.

Time's gentle touch on the waxen brow,
Where dreams are hushed, and hearts avow.
In flames we trust, through joy and blame,
The serene embers of forgotten tales.

Chapters unread in the pages worn,
In silence thick, our hearts are drawn.
The fire's dance is a timeless game,
The serene embers of forgotten tales.

Each crackle a verse, each spark a sigh,
A bridge to moments that dared to fly.
In memories' warmth, our spirits aim,
The serene embers of forgotten tales.

Dancing Lights in the Ashen Realm

In a world draped in a smoky veil,
Dancing lights weave a luminous trail.
Ghosts of warmth in the cold surround,
Dancing lights in the ashen realm.

Flickers of hope through the darkened mist,
In every shimmer, there's something missed.
We grasp at dreams, though shadows overwhelm,
Dancing lights in the ashen realm.

Each spark a heartbeat, alive and bold,
Stories in motion, ready to unfold.
Through the stillness, courageous hearts helm,
Dancing lights in the ashen realm.

Twilight's embrace, a gentle push,
Guiding us forth in the twilight hush.
With every flicker, our spirits overwhelm,
Dancing lights in the ashen realm.

In the frail glow, connections arise,
A fusion of dreams under starry skies.
In dark's embrace, we fiercely overwhelm,
Dancing lights in the ashen realm.

Wings of Ember and Ethereal Light

On wings of ember, we drift and soar,
Chasing the echoes of dreams we adore.
In a realm of magic, we take our flight,
Wings of ember and ethereal light.

Through the twilight skies, our spirits gleam,
A tapestry woven from voices' dream.
Guided by constellations so bright,
Wings of ember and ethereal light.

Each feather a whisper of love untold,
Carried by breezes, both tender and bold.
In unity's dance, we feel the height,
Wings of ember and ethereal light.

Embers arise from the flames of our past,
Carrying stories of shadows cast.
With hearts entwined, we take our flight,
Wings of ember and ethereal light.

In the gentle night, where dreams collide,
We find our haven, our hearts as guide.
In this luminous dance, we claim our right,
Wings of ember and ethereal light.

The Radiant Flight of Echoing Dreams

In twilight's grace, whispers rise,
Dancing shadows, painted skies.
With every breath, the pulse of night,
Dreams take wing, in radiant flight.

Stars ignite, as wishes gleam,
In the heart, ignites the dream.
Echoes of laughter, soft and clear,
Carry the hopes that linger near.

Through valleys wide, and mountains high,
Visions soar, forever nigh.
In silence spoken, secrets unfold,
In echoes bright, the tales are told.

Lifting spirits, warm embrace,
In this realm, we find our place.
Amidst the clouds, we chase our fate,
Together in dreams, we navigate.

So let us rise, on wings of light,
Embracing the glow of endless night.
A tapestry woven, in hues of gold,
The radiant flight, as dreams unfold.

Aetherial Glows Amidst Fiery Tales

In realms of dusk, where starlight weaves,
Fiery tales, the heart believes.
Aetherial glows, a guiding flame,
Whispering softly, calling our name.

With each flicker, the stories swirl,
In every ember, mysteries unfurl.
Passion ignites, a fervent dance,
Entwined in fate, lost in chance.

Through ancient woods, the shadows play,
Painting legends in the fray.
A chorus rises, bold and bright,
Aetherial glows, consuming the night.

In the fire's breath, we find our song,
In every echo, where we belong.
Guided by light, we share our lore,
A tapestry woven, forevermore.

So gather close, and feel the heat,
In fiery tales, our hearts will meet.
Aetherial glow, where dreams take flight,
Amidst the embers, we'll find the light.

Phoenix Flight: The Light of Echoing Hope

From ashes born, the phoenix soars,
In splendid hues, it breaks all doors.
In flames of gold, rebirth takes shape,
Echoing hope, our dreams escape.

Through trials faced, the fire's grace,
Ignites the spirit, leads the race.
With every flap, a promise made,
In the light, the shadows fade.

Around the sun, the wings unfurl,
In radiant circles, the visions whirl.
From depths of sorrow, to heights so steep,
In fiery embrace, our hearts shall leap.

With every rise, we rise anew,
In brilliant colors, a vibrant hue.
Phoenix flight, a guiding beam,
In the dance of life, we chase the dream.

So let the flame, your spirit guide,
In hopes so true, let love abide.
Through trials and triumphs, we find our way,
The light of hope, forever stay.

The Shining Legacy of Flame and Echo

In silence kept, the stories glow,
Whispers of flame, from long ago.
A legacy forged, in hearts so bright,
In echoes soft, it takes its flight.

Across the years, like rivers flow,
Wisdom gathered, in sacred glow.
Flame and echo, hand in hand,
A tale unfolds, across the land.

With every spark, a memory sings,
In the chorus, the past still clings.
Shining brightly, through darkened days,
A legacy found in myriad ways.

In the warmth of fire, we ignite,
The echoes dance in the soft twilight.
Stories woven, in threads of gold,
The shining legacy, forever told.

So cherish the flame, and heed its call,
In every echo, we rise and fall.
Unity's strength in every heart,
The shining legacy, our sacred art.

A Blaze of Remembrance in the Night

In the dark, memories glow,
Flickering thoughts start to flow.
Whispers of the past ignite,
Dancing softly in the night.

Guided by the stars above,
Echoes blend with dreams of love.
Each flame tells a tale untold,
Burning brightly, fierce and bold.

Through the shadows, light will bridge,
Sparks of hope beneath the ridge.
In the stillness, we ignite,
A blaze of warmth to hold us tight.

With each ember, a heart's sigh,
Moments cherished never die.
In the night, our spirits soar,
A blaze of light forevermore.

Together with the moonlit view,
We find strength in what is true.
As time flows, we weave our thread,
In remembrance, we are led.

Resplendent Flames of the Skybound Spirit

High above, the colors blend,
A dance of fire that won't end.
Resplendent flames, they leap and twirl,
In the vastness, bright jewels whirl.

Spirits soaring, hearts ablaze,
Guided by the cosmic gaze.
Each flicker holds a whispered prayer,
In the night, we feel them there.

Celestial warmth washes our fears,
In the glow, we shed our tears.
Skybound flames, oh, how they sing,
Of unity and hope they bring.

In the silence of the night,
Every spark ignites our light.
With each heartbeat, we ascend,
In resplendent dreams, we blend.

Together, we embrace the fire,
Igniting a collective desire.
Soaring high, we set our aim,
In the sky, we play the game.

The Bright Symphony of Ascending Ashes

From the wood, the embers rise,
A symphony beneath the skies.
Notes of warmth in twilight's hush,
In the still, we feel the rush.

Ashen trails of dreams set free,
Each note whispers, 'Come, follow me.'
Through the darkness, hope will shine,
A bright path that feels divine.

In the air, a melody flows,
With every spark, our spirit grows.
The harmony of night unfolds,
In the heat, our hearts take hold.

As ashes curl and drift away,
New beginnings greet the day.
Each moment, bright with love's embrace,
In this symphony, we find our place.

Together, we create the sound,
Of rising hopes all around.
In the quiet, let it thrash,
The bright symphony of ashes' crash.

Glimmering Futures Born from the Fire

Fires burn with purpose true,
Glimmers shine in shades anew.
From the heat, bright futures rise,
In the warmth, we seek the skies.

With each spark, a dream ignites,
Guiding us through distant nights.
Visions dance like flames in flight,
Carving paths into the light.

Born from struggles and the strife,
Fires forge a vibrant life.
In the embers, promise gleams,
Whispering soft about our dreams.

As we walk the path ahead,
Following where the fire led,
Hope unfurls in each new morn,
Glimmering futures, bright and worn.

Together, we chase the blaze,
Through the shadows, through the haze.
In the fire, we become whole,
Glimmering futures, one shared soul.

9 781805 595311